Animals on the Farm

Pigs

by Wendy Strobel Dieker

Bullfrog
Books

Ideas for Parents and Teachers

Bullfrog Books give children practice reading nonfiction at the earliest levels. Repetition, familiar words, and photos support early readers.

Before Reading

- Discuss the cover photo with the class. What does it tell them?
- Look at the picture glossary together. Read and discuss the words.

Read the Book

- "Walk" through the book and look at the photos. Let the child ask questions.
- Read the book to the child, or have him or her read independently.

After Reading

- Prompt the child to think more. Ask: Would you like to raise pigs? Would a pig make a good pet? Why or why not?

Bullfrog Books are published by Jump!
5357 Penn Avenue South
Minneapolis, MN 55419
www.jumplibrary.com

Library of Congress Cataloging-in-Publication Data
Dieker, Wendy Strobel.
 Pigs / by Wendy Strobel Dieker.
    p. cm. -- (Bullfrog books: animals on the farm)
 Includes index.
 Summary: "A pig narrates this photo-illustrated book describing the body parts and behavior of pigs on a farm. Includes photo glossary"—Provided by publisher.
 ISBN 978-1-62031-005-2 (hardcover)
 1. Swine as pets--Juvenile literature. 2. Swine-Behavior--Juvenile literature. I. Title.
 SF395.6.D54 2013
 636.4--dc23

                          2012008422

Photo Credits: Alamy, 12-13, 20-21; Corbis, 5; Dreamstime.com, 1, 4, 8, 9, 10, 14, 23bl, 23br, 24; Getty, 6-7, 11, 16-17, 22; iStockphoto, 23tl; National Geographic Stock, 14-15; Shutterstock, 3 (all), 7, 17, 18, 18-19, 23tr

Series Editor: Rebecca Glaser
Series Designer: Ellen Huber
Production: Chelsey Luther

Printed in the United States of America at Corporate Graphics in North Mankato, Minnesota
7-2012/ PO 1121
10 9 8 7 6 5 4 3 2 1

Table of Contents

Pigs on the Farm

I am a pig.
I live on a farm.

Do you see my tiny eyes?
I can't see well.

Do you see
my curly tail?

The farmer cut it short when I was a piglet.

Do you see my floppy ears?

10

They shade
my eyes.

Do you see me
roll in the mud?

Mud keeps me cool.

snout

Do you see my snout?
I dig with it.
I find bugs to eat. Yum!

Do you hear
me grunting?

I smell food!

The farmer
feeds me pellets.

Do you see my thick body?

I can push over fences.

I need a strong pen.

I am smart.
I learned to
open the gate.

20

Pig on the loose!

Parts of a Pig

snout
The long front part of an animal's head; it includes the nose and mouth.

tail
A part that sticks out at the back of an animal's body.

hoof
The hard covering of an animal's foot.

Picture Glossary

grunt
To make a deep, gruff sound.

pen
A fenced-in area where a pig stays.

pellets
Food made of grain and minerals that farm animals eat.

piglet
A baby pig.

Index

To Learn More

Learning more is as easy as 1, 2, 3.

1) Go to www.factsurfer.com

2) Enter "pig" into the search box.

3) Click the "Surf" button to see a list of websites.

With factsurfer.com, finding more information is just a click away.